Mortimer Collins

The British Birds

A Communication From the Ghost of Aristophanes

Mortimer Collins

The British Birds
A Communication From the Ghost of Aristophanes

ISBN/EAN: 9783337002275

Printed in Europe, USA, Canada, Australia, Japan

Cover: Foto ©Thomas Meinert / pixelio.de

More available books at **www.hansebooks.com**

THE BRITISH BIRDS.

A COMMUNICATION FROM THE

GHOST OF ARISTOPHANES.

BY

MORTIMER COLLINS.

LONDON:

THE PUBLISHING COMPANY, LIMITED,

7, QUALITY COURT, CHANCERY LANE.

MDCCCLXXII.

TO

MISS LOUISA COURT,

OF

CASTLEMANS.

———o———

Lady, whose eyes oft deign to look
Over my careless rhyming words,
Use as you will this tiny book,
In which I treat of British Birds....
Some plumaged dusk, some bright of hue,
And never one so fair as you.

M. C.

THE BRITISH BIRDS.

A COMMUNICATION FROM THE

GHOST OF ARISTOPHANES.

ΤΑ ΤΟΥ ΔΡΑΜΑΤΟΣ ΠΡΟΣΩΠΑ.

EUELPIDES.

PEISTHETAIRUS.

TOM TIT.

KING ROC.

PROCNE.

SENTINEL.

IRIS.

MAN OF THE ADELPHI.

BROW ⎫
BEARD ⎬ *Three Poets.*
HAIR ⎭

PROTOPLAST ⎫
GERM ⎪
⎬ *Four Philosophers.*
GORILLA ⎪
SEWING MACHINE ⎭

LAETUSLAPIS ⎫
BISNOTUS ⎬ *Three Statesmen.*
LACHRIMAE ⎭

B

"Scena exhibet agrestem, saxosam, fruticibus et arbustis impli-
citam regionem; in una parte cernitur saltus: propius rupes,
Epopis sedes, Euelpides graculum, Peisthetairus cornicem gestans,
ut viam ad aves monstrant, diversis partibus incedunt, ita tamen ut
colloqui inter se possent."—WIELAND.

PEISTHETAIRUS, the hero of the play, is the "persuasive com-
panion"; EUELPIDES, his follower, is the "cheery comrade." They
are Greek types, twenty-three centuries old, of Quixote and Sancho
Panza, of Pickwick and Sam Weller.

In giving what is not precisely either a "transcript" or a parody
of *The Birds*, I shall often try to imitate the masterly rhythms of
John Hookham Frere.

EUELPIDES *to his Jackdaw.*

Is it that tree there, Jack, we have to reach?

PEISTHETAIRUS.

My croaking raven says we should return.

EUELPIDES.

And so our journey's at an end, confound it!

PEISTHETAIRUS.

It looks much like it. Think of my being fool enough
To tramp a thousand miles with a croaking bird
As guide, philosopher, and friend!

EUELPIDES.

Mine caws...
And is the cause why I have worn my boots out,
And my feet too, and laid in the rheumatics
For all my life at the least.   Why did you send me
To buy wise birds there in Saint Martin's Lane...
Birds that have swindled us into such a journey?
If ever I get back again I'll twist
The neck of every talking bird I see,
Even of my old Granny's parrot, who surprised us
So much, we always called him Mister Attorney.
I'd rather trust the beasts in Ratcliffe Highway
Than any bird, hereafter.

PEISTHETAIRUS.

Ha, an omen!
My raven points to that grotesque rock-archway
That looks like a colossal birdcage.   Take
A flint and throw at the door.

[*The door is opened.   A* TOM TIT *comes out.*

EUELPIDES.

Ho, ho, my little friend in the blue and yellow!
Who, pray, are you?

TOM TIT.

The great King's servitor.

EUELPIDES.

Great King! a queer place this for a great King!
What may be this aërial monarch's name?

TOM TIT.

King Roc, you featherless birds of evil omen!
Not to know him argues yourselves unknown,
As once was said by bird of sable feather.

EUELPIDES.

The Raven croaks a fearsome note : my Jack
Just puts his clever clerical head aside,
Looking askant at all this nonsense.

PEISTHETAIRUS.

Ay,

Yet was King Roc a mighty potentate,
Mentioned in old Arabian chronicles,
Who carried off a very famous sailor,
One Sindbad of the Sea, and let him down
Into a Valley of Diamonds.

EUELPIDES.

Diämonds!
Perhaps this King will do the same for us.
But is it veritable history?

PEISTHETAIRUS.

As true as Whittaker's Pinnock's Goldsmith...

EUELPIDES.

Whew!
Don't mention that : it makes me hear again
The mastigophorous preceptor's roar.
...But see, there's something moving.   O Tom Tit!
Don't let your mighty master's giant claw
Obliterate us from the world of air.

[*Enter* KING ROC.   TOM TIT *perches on his enormous crest.*

EUELPIDES.

A dreadful apparition!   King of birds,
If kings on earth were just as unmistakable,
I'd have been loyal.

KING ROC.

                    Were you not loyal then?
I'll have no democrats here.   Tell him, Tom Tit,
The way we serve them.

TOM TIT.

                    Tie them up to a tree,
Stript of their rags, and all the little birds
Come in their myriads, peck their horny hides,
Just as a robin redbreast pecks a bone,
Twittering a mockery of their eloquence.

EUELPIDES.

Goodness!   Poor Dilke! he must not come this way.
But I am truly loyal, your Majesty;
And always have been loyal, and always will.

King Roc.

If loyal, be true in speech. Whence come ye twain?

Euelpides.

From the immaculate Island, which contains
The greatest city and the grandest brains;
Which rules the sea—or did ere Nelson died;
Which keeps the peace in Europe—or has tried ;
Which has so wise a folk in streets and schools,
That only those who govern it are fools ;
Which sinks great war-ships ......

King Roc.

     Stop your wretched jargon.
We birds care nothing for nonentities.
Sometimes my swallows, easy travellers,
Who rather like to haunt the eaves of men,
Gossip a little of their follies...tell
How they delight to scold at one another,
And call it Politics...delight to kill
With engines cowards can use, and call it War.
If you were really proud of this poor Island,

Why are you here ? Come, answer straight at once,
Or I'll suspend you over space, and drop you
Into the unfathomable sapphire, where
You'll fall, fall, fall unto the Day of Doom,—
Or till you meet a comet.

EUELPIDES.

[*Aside.*]   Worse than Hawkins. (*a*)

PEISTHETAIRUS.

[*Interposing.*] My herald is a fool, most noble King...
Tailor by trade, of garrulous Tooley Street,
Accustomed much to speak in Hatton Garden—
Enamoured of his rather husky voice
And broken English.

KING ROC.

Well then, who are you ?
What want you here ?

PEISTHETAIRUS.

Mine is a great vocation.

I am architect of Castles in the Air,
And now desire to build a city there
By aid of the Birds, and for the Birds to dwell in,
And reässert their antique sovereignty—
And from that Capital rule both gods and men.

KING ROC.

You're a remarkable man.

EUELPIDES.

(*Aside.*)   Remarked too much :
He's been a bear, a bull, a guinea-pig ;
Promoter hath he been, and liquidator :
He hath been architect of everything —
Save his own luck ...... and mine.

PEISTHETAIRUS.

                    A moment mark
The noble site on which you have to build,
And your stupendous isolation.   Why,
The gods being troublesome, they dare not pass,
Except by treaty, through this city of yours ;

c

And you can stop their hourly provender
Of prayers and incense-fumes.

KING ROC.

A grand idea!

PEISTHETAIRUS.

Then don't you see the double interception?
Men, your worst enemies from very boyhood,
Who harry your nests for fun, who dine upon you;
Who kill the loveliest of you carelessly,
To crest the crestless featherless she-bipeds,
The girls, who grow not nor are worth a feather,
Who shut you up in cages for their pleasure,
Being unable to send up their incense,
Will find themselves at quarrel with the gods.
Both sides will suffer.   Zeus will not be able,
Overlooking green Olympian battlements,
To espy some pretty maid all-Danaë.   (*β*)
Poseidaon will lose communication
With the Great British Lords of the Admiralty,
Who'll thenceforth lose their freedom from mistakes,

Their high administrative wisdom.   Rothschilds
Will miss their Plutus.   All will be a chaos
On high Olympus and in the nether world,
Until both gods and men make full submission,
Pay tribute, own that they are subject nations,
And evermore abstain from all aggression.

KING ROC.

Hurrah, my friend !   I like the fancy mightily.
Where learnt you it ?

PEISTHETAIRUS.

                    The thing is done on earth
In a degree.   We English hold the way
From our own island to our East dominions,
By keeping in our hands some small strong places
Won from our foes.   But your municipality
Will be the capital of earth and heaven,
And dominate two worlds.

KING ROC.

                    A noble notion !

I'll summon all the nation of the Birds :
You shall harangue them.

PEISTHETAIRUS.

Will they understand me ?

KING ROC.

Birds understand all languages.

PEISTHETAIRUS.

But how
Can you bring round you, from the infinite sphere,
All birds that fly or swim ?   I see no cannon,
No belfry tower......not even a brass band.

KING ROC.

Are we barbarians ?   My nightingale
Is heard throughout the air with delicate throat.
Bell-jangle, cannon-clang, and bugle-scream
Are hideous discord.   Now I'll summon her
Harken ! ......

α

Cease thou from sleep, my fellow ! (γ)
Pour sacred hymns forth from thy throat divine !
In plaintive numbers mellow
Wailing lamented Itys, thine and mine,
With tones that swell and float
Out of thy tawny throat.

β

Clear the sweet sound is going
Through shady woodbine to the throne of Zeus.
Thine eloquent anguish flowing
Makes golden-haired Apollo cry " The Deuce !
The loveliest voice I've heard
Belongs to that sweet Bird."
[*The Nightingale replies from the grove.*

PEISTHETAIRUS.

O fluting absolute ! Apollo may follow,
But this sweet hidden bird will beat him hollow.
She sings with notes that vary yet never vary
In her dim green delicious woodland sanctuary.
Will she not sing again ?

PROCNE *sings:*

α

O is there not pleasure and pain ?

　　And pleasure is pain's undoing.

And sunshine also and rain ?

　　And rain the sun's sweet wooing.

For me, I sing in the shade

For the man who loves and the maid,

Who are pure and unafraid

　　Of the old old love-pursuing.

β

What lady has not heard,

　　When summer scents are strongest,

The fluting voluble bird

　　Whose accents dwell the longest ?

What silent secret copse

Devoid of my music-drops ?

At the inn where young Love stops

　　You shall never meet the wrong guest.

γ

We must all of us love...and love

Is of life the perfect issue.
Love not! ... the gods above
    Nor the fools beneath will miss you.
Love! ... truly and void of crime,
And the haggard hand of Time
Will be foiled by your light love-rhyme
    Though writ upon lighter tissue.

δ

I am the Nightingale!
    The gods...I am rather loth of them...
Cannot stay my old love-tale:
    As for men...I hate the sloth of them.
I sing for the Poet who cries—
" I love thy breast and eyes
And thy soul that never dies."
    Gods and men! One Poet's worth both
    of them.

PEISTHETAIRUS.

That's not an ordinary London metre
Of Tate and Brady or of Doctor Watts;

Or of the music-halls. That bird can sing.
Not much experienced in nightingales,
Though once they kept me broad awake all night, (δ)
I like that throat-rich foliage-sojourner,
That gods-and-men-despising poet-lover.
And it is charming that she will charm, we are told,
All birds that soar in air and merge in sea,
All birds that splash in Blackmore's own Caÿster, (ε)
All birds that traffic over ocean's waste,
All birds that man eats, all birds that eat men,
All birds whatsoever from peak and·copse and river,
And bring them to hear the great haranguer's clangour.

King Roc.

                    Wait !
Don't be a fool and fight with Fate !
You, who have wasted many words,
Know not the marvellous power of birds.
Epopopopopopopopopopoi !   .   (ζ)
That's my ornithic strong *Ahoy !*
          That's the thing...
The well-known cry of their mighty King.

They have heard my Queen, the Nightingale,
Tell in sweet old notes her old sweet tale :
My summons settles the business. Soon
Darkness will cover the Sun and the Moon.

PEISTHETAIRUS.

By Zeus, an excellent notion, King,
You can darken earth with innumerous wing ;
That's another point wherein you've odds
Against weak men and weaker gods.

KING ROC.

You are suggestive. Well, there'll be some merriment,
Their coming now will test the queer experiment.
Astronomers will swear 'tis an eclipse.
Truth always drops from mathematic lips.

CHORUS.

No more words !
Now come the Birds !
Multitudinous...
Sky imbued in us

D

Shut up sunset
By our onset.
Mighty muster,
Cluster, bluster,
Some with lustre...
Pheasants and Partridges,
Far beyond cartridges...
Woodcock whose trail
Will never avail...
Larks in the *mêlée*
Seeking for Shelley...
Tom Tits that lie
With feet to the sky...
Owls that, though wise,   (η)
Like scratching on eyes :
Royal mountain Eagle,
Every inch regal ;
Peak-haunting Vulture,
Bird of less culture...
Hawk Heron-hated,
And Heron Hawk-baited ;
Multitudes vast,
The sky's overcast.

EUELPIDES.

I say!

Let's run away.

Air darkens.

Who harkens

When every bird

One ever heard,

That æther stirred,

Says every word,

That ever occurred,

To bird's mind?

The sky's lined!

The wind's hurried!

The brain's flurried!

O why

Ever did I

Leave my sweet

Nasty fusty musty fooly Tooley Street?

I wish I was a boy once more,

And had a bow and arrows;

I think to-night I'd lock the door,
And eat a pie of sparrows.

KING ROC.

Well friend, our birds are here, enough of them.
Make your harangue.

PEISTHETAIRUS.

Enough of them, you say.
To govern such a mighty marvellous nation
Is a great destiny.   We human folk
Are far too much alike.   Thus man from woman
Is known by ugliness of attire in the one,
And tawdry finery in the other.   You
Have natural loveliness on both sides, but give
To the nobler sex the fairer feather.

KING ROC.

Yes,
Your system's strange.   But a most ancient Roc
Who taught me centuries ago quaint lore,
Said that you hid yourselves in wrappages

Of wool of sheep and web of worm, because
Your natural ugliness would drive you mad
If you perceived it often.

PEISTHETAIRUS.

It may be.
I don't remember, in our great philosophers,
Any such theory: Huxley, Darwin, Tyndall,
Stuart Mill, whom I have studied carefully,
Do not lay down the principle, and therefore
I must suspend my judgment.

KING ROC.

You believe
Nothing but what those men with creaking names
Tell you... say what they say, and call it wisdom!

PEISTHETAIRUS.

Well, they are very wise.

KING ROC.

Why you're a parrot...

A parrot without excuse of gorgeous plumage.
It has been noticed in the realm of birds
The ugliest parrots always talked the best,
The handsomest the greatest nonsense.   Well,
We tolerate folly from a brilliant bird
As from a charming woman.   But you, sir, you—
A parrot-man without a speck of the rainbow
Anywhere in your plumage.   I advise you
Not to annoy the Birds, the heirs of knowledge,
Who traffic 'twixt two spheres unceasingly,
With small ridiculous notions second-hand...
Notions in Greece exploded long ago,
When I was young, and Plato yet unborn.

PEISTHETAIRUS.

Pardon, King Roc.   We mortals have our faults :
You birds have none save that you will not hold
Your sovereign and supreme position.   Yours
Is that great realm, the uninvadable Air.
Herein now let me build a mighty city,
Based upon cloud and turreted with fire,
Which wandering travellers shall see in sunsets,

See its broad streets, its countless palaces,
See the cloud-river winding through the town,
And wish it were their fate to dwell therein.

King Roc.

Well, talk to the Assembly of the Birds,
And prove yourself no parrot.   They will listen.

Peisthetairus.

Birds! who are stronger and greater and wiser
Than Zeus the immortal, than me your adviser!
Who flew in the æther before there was earth,
And laid your smooth eggs before Chronos's birth...

Chorus.

This man is no miser
Of wisdom and mirth.

Peisthetairus.

Birds! whom I love for your song and your sweet-
ness,
I come with a scheme that shall give you complete-
ness,

When with it the panic-struck universe rings,
Gods are baffled, men puzzled, and you are its Kings!

CHORUS.

This man has some neatness
In putting such things.

PEISTHETAIRUS.

Birds! that are fearless of lout's gun and lad's stone!
Birds! that ne'er listened to rascally Rad's tone!
Your monarch will never be driven half mad
By the rout and the Rad and the lout and the lad.

CHORUS.

He alludes to one Gladstone,
Whose fate's very sad.

PEISTHETAIRUS.

Birds who aspire may more splendour afar win,
Or lovelier life in some happier star win :
But ye always were birds ... and no fancy escapes
To picture your fathers of horriblest shapes.

CHORUS.

Go earthward for Darwin ...
Great grandson of apes!

PEISTHETAIRUS.

Birds! ye soar high in the regions of Wonder,
Hear the winds' warfare, and fly through the thunder;
But from softest of sow's ear you never made silk,
Nor fed a young child upon house-pigeon's milk.

CHORUS.

Does he hint at the blunder
Of Baronet Dilke?

KING ROC.

You're getting enigmatical, my friend,
And prolix, and exhausted of idea,
All human faults, unknown among the Birds.
Come to the point without this roundabout.
I'm tired, and want my dinner... an elephant
All white, brought yesterday through air from Siam.

E

EUELPIDES (*aside to* PEISTHETAIRUS).

Don't elephants want hanging ?

PEISTHETAIRUS.

No : but *you* do.
[*Then he proceeds to harangue.*]
Birds, your annoyances fill me with pity,
Wherefore I urge you to build a great city,
Steadfast and firm on the cloud-rift that lies
Here, between earth and the hyaline skies.

CHORUS.

Isn't he witty ?
And isn't he wise ?

PEISTHETAIRUS.

Seeing before me the noblest of races
Holding the best of unoccupied spaces,
Not to induce them their power to prolong
Would be exceedingly wicked and wrong.

CHORUS.

Faith ! there are traces
Of sense in his song.

PEISTHETAIRUS.

Fearless you'll be, as the eagle of Merlin,
As to big London, pert Paris, grim Berlin:
Treaties enforce with them, banish your cares,
Terminate shooting and cages and snares.

CHORUS.

O what a whirl in
Poor human affairs!

PEISTHETAIRUS.

England's great statesmen 'twill be a sad blow to.
Laws they can't make unless yearly they flow to
Heathery highlands and shoot down the grouse.
Eating them yields them a little more nous.

CHORUS.

Who now will go to
The Parliament House?

PEISTHETAIRUS.

Are you decided then? Quite undivided then

Will you by my sole direction be guided then ?
Every species of featherclad fowls...
Eagles, wrens, attagens, cormorants, owls ?

Chorus.

We *are* decided then !
Now for the trowels.

King Roc.

Eloquent friend, my presence here would surely be
 irrelevant :
So I shall to my palace go, and dine upon my elephant.
A baby one, all white, it is ... an exquisite comestible.
Than your superb harangue I hope to find it more
 digestible.

Peisthetairus.

Your Majesty, I much regret.

King Roc.

     Regret is an hysteric old.
(If he begins regretting my mammal will be very cold.)

Just set a million birds at work : talk on and don't
   diminish it.

To 'scape the rancour of your tongue by sunset they
   will finish it.

So go ahead, and let me know...and when the news
   you're bringing me,

Asleep, after a dinner rare, sweet Procne will be
   singing me.

> [*Exeunt* PEISTHETAIRUS *and* EUELPIDES *to draw
> plans of the city, while the birds fly off in
> many directions to find building materials.
> When* PEISTHETAIRUS *and* EUELPIDES *re-
> appear, the former has been changed to a
> game cock and the latter to a bantam cock.*

PEISTHETAIRUS.

Crow !

EUELPIDES.

I'll crow,
And I'll fight also :
Though you're rather too heavy for me you know,
We were yesterday werry respectable Cockneys,

With the Wapping slouch and the Rotherhithe knock-
  knees;
And now we're a brace of birds whose look
Would delight the heart of a capable cook.

PEISTHETAIRUS.

Bantam you, but I am game,
  And don't regret my London :
For I found that fuliginous city tame
  With my creditors every one done.
But now my destiny's fulfilled,
And a marvellous City I mean to build,
A City so fair, so strong, so strange,
Nothing shall touch it in Air's wide range :
A City of light, of purity, mirth,
Life and love, untouched on earth—
Even while I speak, my birds are at it.
Even while I speak, old Zeus cries " *Drat it !* "
For he knows when we've set this town·in the blue
The gods will have no work to do.

PARABASIS.

Comedy meaneth sweet play in a village :

There we have tillage, but who tills the air?
O what a pity that Atmosphere City
Hasn't foundation that's likely to wear!
Found it, O Founder! and don't let it flounder,
Would it were sounder, and perfectly safe:
Then its philosophers often would toss over
Its battlements words to make wiseacres chafe.
For listen, I beg...the world is an egg
Laid by a bird of amazing enormity,
And the people who walk on its surface, and talk,
Are insects minute, and of curious deformity.
Great Zeus as he lists guides all that exists,
And makes no mistakes though mistakers mistake him:
Apollo flies swift through the dazzling sun-drift;
Right happy the poet who dare overtake him.

Hand a round silver bowl to stir mystical porridge in !...
Now shall you know of all creatures the origin.
Murk Midnight, the only existence at first,
Felt extremely unhappy, and ready to burst,
And with pains indescribable grew half delirious,
,...... And at last laid an egg ......,

.... Which turned out to be Sirius.
Well, Sirius did not his energies smother,
But gave light—and astonished his murky old mother.
Astronomic conception proceeded : the wiseac-
-res wonder what else we'd have done with Sir Isaac.
Since Sirius existed and sparkled and twisted,
Folk grew telescope-wristed and compasses-fisted,
Whence somehow, in time, we became solar-systed.
Then the Earth, which is not such a bad sort of planet,
Was built somehow or other on basis of granite ;
By a glory of air it was suddenly fed,
As if with some marvellous deity wed :
Its woodlands grew green and its rivers grew clear,
Its birds sang delicious soft songs to the ear ;
And its lords and its ladies who walked in the land
Had a splendour beyond what the rest understand,
Stood erect, and were masters and mistresses too,
And used the great motto, " *I do what I do :* "
And they used one more motto, in meaning above
The one I have quoted, " *I love whom I love.*"
And the Earth knew its lords, and was anxious to seem
A slave of some service : and so there was steam,

There were ugly light-pictures, and telegraph-cables,
And many a clever device which enables
Your aunt or your cousin, your uncle or you,
To do what you really would rather not do.

But what is it all? When the great world began
It had but one issue or terminus...MAN.
Worth while to create this small orb...and exult...
If nothing but SHAKESPEARE had been the result.
Worth while—but on pain of becoming a bore
It probably is not worth while to say more.

     [PEISTHETAIRUS *and* EUELPIDES *are at work on the
       plan of the City. There is a flutter of wings
       and a blaze of colour. Enter a* SENTINEL.

SENTINEL.

My lord, a coloured creature from Olympus
Has just burst through our fortifications. See!
'Tis like a sudden rainbow underneath.

PEISTHETAIRUS.

Send half a dozen falcons off at once :
We'll soon know what it means.

[*Enter* IRIS *in charge of the hawks that have
captured her. She is of course (I use
Frere's words, vol. ii. p.* 192) *attired in all
the colours of the rainbow with abundance
of lappets and streamers.*

EUELPIDES.

Master, this highflyer,
Looks like Vibgyor.   (θ)
She'd say to any goosy swain, Bo !
Carrying all the colours of the rainbow.

PEISTHETAIRUS.

You hussy !
You're Jessy,   (ı)
The naughty and dressy,
Whom Dante Rossetti
Called lovelily pretty,
For meshing poor ninnies
With Danaë guineas.
Off with her to Bridewell !
Rainbow her hide well !
That's the way to serve goddesses
In vibgyor bodices.

EUELPIDES.

She's rather a nice sample of Olympus.
You need not be so harsh.

PEISTHETAIRUS.

Euelpides!
I mean to make this City in the Air,
A moral and a model city.

EUELPIDES.

O!

[*Enter a gentleman from somewhere near the
Adelphi, whose vocation is to catch capitalists
and find brilliant names for new companies.
He carries a blue bag full of prospectuses,
and wears an atrociously bad hat.*

MAN OF THE ADELPHI.

Your servant, sir.

PEISTHETAIRUS.

Why, by the powers, who's this?
I've seen this seedy ragamuffin before.

Wasn't he chairman of a joint-stock bank
That I promoted ?   Don't I recollect him
At Rutland Gate, in one of those big houses,
With many servants, horses, carriages,
A billiard-room, a private theatre,
Magnificent plate, and very meagre dinners ?
Yes : that's the man.   I know his unked nose.
But his fair linen and his diamond rings,
And weighty watch-chain, platinum and gold,
That might be cable to a lady's yacht,'
Seem to have gone where limited companies go
When trust in them's unlimited.

                              Your business ?

MAN OF THE ADELPHI.

I am a nomenclator.

PEISTHETAIRUS.

                              Nomenclator !

MAN OF THE ADELPHI.

Yes, I find names for cities, novels, ladies,

New companies, new newspapers, aught new ;
And so I thought you'd give me, say, ten guineas,
To name your fine new city.

Peisthetairus.

      Well, go on.

Man of the Adelphi.

Since London is the centre of the world,
The noblest city ever built by man...

Peisthetairus.

I've read that in the London papers.   Well?

Man of the Adelphi.

Call it New London!

Peisthetairus.

        Lovely thought! O yes!
With a New Piccadilly, New Pall Mall,
New Billiter Lane, New Cripplegate, New Bedlam ;
Why did not such a fancy strike my mind

When I began upon the cloudy strata
My silent smokeless pure policeless city?
You and your brothers of the astute Adelphi,
Need not perplex yourselves to name this City :
It has been named long since.

MAN OF THE ADELPHI.

What name, your Highness?

PEISTHETAIRUS.

And "what's the nearest post-town?" I suppose.
Pooh, pooh, sir, you are troublesome.   This city
Apollo gave to Aristophanes,
What time the jury of the world were only
The Muses and the Graces.   It was named   (x)
Cloud-Cuckoo-City... being based on cloud,
And having, as is customary on earth,
Repetitive cuckoos as its Mayors and Councillors.
So you're anticipated, my good fellow.
Return to the Adelphi.

[*Exit* MAN OF THE ADELPHI.

[*Enter three Poets, all handsome. One hath
    redundant hair, a second redundant beard,
    a third redundant brow. They present a
    letter of introduction from an eminent
    London publisher (whom I am requested
    not to name) stating that they are candidates
    for the important post of Poet Laureate to
    the new Municipality.*

PEISTHETAIRUS (*reflectively*).

Very troublesome,
These inconsiderable interruptions.
Still cormorants are useful, and my friend
The publisher is one.   Wise fishers put
A ring around the throat of that same bird,
And so restrain its swallow.

Gentlemen :
Happy to see you in the Realms of Air.
As yet the worthy Mayor and Aldermen
And Councillors of the Town have not decided
Whether they want a Poet Laureate.
But, if 'twill ease your minds to sing a little,
I'll try and listen.   As my memory

Fails me entirely in regard to names,
Let me without the least discourtesy
Name you by your appearance.   Amorous Naso
Was named from his chief feature.   So I beg
To call you HAIR, and BEARD, and BROW.

THE THREE POETS.

Agreed.

PEISTHETAIRUS.

Who will talk, any more, of the *genus irritabile*
        Vatum ?
What wonder if poets, when the people treat 'em
    shabbily,
        Hate 'em ?
But they don't, they desire to destroy the seeds that
    germinate
        Hatred ;
And their movement has a strong demiurgic deter-
    minate
        Gay tread.
So I'm marvellously fond of Poets when I luckily
        See such :

And my pride is to decide and arrange in order pluckily,

   Three such.

For the topic...as 'tis tropic

Heat at present...perhaps 'twere pleasant

   If each Paladin

   His ballad in

   Put salad in.

But there must be no single metre, please,

That's not allowed by Dr. Guest, of Caius.   (λ)

EUELPIDES.

For this delightful tourney of rhyme I hunger :

Who's to begin, my master ?

PEISTHETAIRUS.

   Why, the younger.

BROW.   ˙

 O cool in the summer is salad,

  And warm in the winter is love ;

 And a poet shall sing you a ballad

  Delicious thereon and thereof.

   G

A singer am I, if no sinner,
   My Muse has a marvellous wing,
And I willingly worship at dinner
      The Sirens of Spring.

Take endive...like love it is bitter ;
   Take beet...for like love it is red :
Crisp leaf of the lettuce shall glitter,
   And cress from the rivulet's bed :
Anchovies foam-born, like the Lady
   Whose beauty has maddened this bard ;
And olives, from groves that are shady ;
      And eggs...boil 'em hard.

EUELPIDES.

If Aphrodite has maddened that young bard,
There's method in his madness and his salad,
And a nice swing in his rhythm.   Who next, sir ?

PEISTHETAIRUS.

BEARD.

BEARD.

Waitress, with eyes so marvellous black,
  And the blackest possible lustrous gay tress,
This is the month of the Zodiac
  When I want a pretty deft-handed waitress.
Bring a china bowl, you merry young soul;
  Bring anything green, from worsted to celery ;
Bring pure olive-oil, from Italy's soil...
  Then your china bowl we'll well array.
When the time arrives chip choicest chives,
  And administer quietly chili and capsicum...
(Young girls do not quite know what's what
  Till as a Poet into their laps I come).
Then a lobster fresh as fresh can be
  (When it screams in the pot I feel a murderer) ;
After which I fancy we
  Shall want a few bottles of Heidseck or Roederer.

EUELPIDES.

Most parenthetical poet ! But I like
BEARD better far than BROW.

PEISTHETAIRUS.

Now summon HAIR.

HAIR.

King Arthur, growing very tired indeed
Of wild Tintagel, now that Launcelot
Had gone to Jersey or to Jericho,
And there was nobody to make a rhyme,
And Cornish girls were christened Jennifer,
And the Round Table had grown rickety,
Said unto Merlin (who had been asleep
For a few centuries in Broceliande,
But woke, and had a bath, and felt refreshed) :
" What shall I do to pull myself together ? "
Quoth Merlin, " Salad is the very thing,
And you can get it at the *Cheshire Cheese.*"
King Arthur went there : verily, I believe
That he has dined there every day since then.
Have you not marked the portly gentleman
In his cool corner, with his plate of greens ?
The great knight Launcelot prefers the *Cock,*
Where port is excellent (in pints), and waiters

Are portlier than kings, and steaks are tender,
And poets have been known to meditate...
Ox-fed orating ominous octastichs.

EUELPIDES.

That's the best poetry I ever heard :
Let HAIR be Laureate of the City of 'Air.

PEISTHETAIRUS.

The question will be left to the Town Council,
Who, I may tell you, gentlemen, have only
Two wishes in the world, two noble wishes,
Two splendid and stupendous wishes, which
Will quite immortalize Cloud-Cuckoo-Town.
One is to get as visitor some member
Of the Royal Family that rule the Air,
To lay our modest small foundation stone ;
The other, that whoever shall be Mayor
Shall receive knighthood. Now, you gentlemen,
Masters complete of the Vernacular,
Who drive in a tandem-cart both Rhyme and Rhythm,
Oft doubtful which is preferable as leader ;

Oft finding both with bit between their teeth,
Ready to bolt; oft wondering whether Rhythm
The stallion is as bad as Rhyme the mare —
I have one word to say to you, one only.
Wait till we've got a jolly sort of Mayor —
A very prosperous and portly grocer;
Add aldermen a trifle thinner, not much;   (μ)
Councillors, as behoves their lower standing,
Of build more meagre, yet by no means lean
(Curved medium of municipal aldermen);
Add also an ingenious Town Clerk,
A clever Mephistopheles-attorney,
Salaried at six hundred pounds a year,
And adding thrice the money in his bills,
Which, when presented, the subservient Council
Don't audit, but transform the pounds to guineas ...
When we have reached this exquisite climax, this
Municipal elysium, come all three
Poets; recite as you have now recited;
And I will guarantee, whatever happens,
That you shall have your railway fares and dinners.

[*Exeunt Poets.*

[*Enter a great number of philosophers, mostly queer in appearance. One slightly resembles a Gorilla, another a Germ, a third a Protoplast, a fourth a Sewing-machine. All four, not to mention several minor philosophers, talk in rigorous defiance of the laws of logic and grammar.* PEISTHETAIRUS *meanwhile smokes a cigar.*

PROTOPLAST.

I am protoplastic : this should be Protopolis...
First city in order, not of time but brain.
Will you accept the positivist creed,
Which shows that man is true divinity ?
If so, I'll lecture to you.

PEISTHETAIRUS.

Pleasant notion !

CHORUS.

α

Life and the universe show spontaneity :
Down with ridiculous notions of Deity !

Churches and creeds are all lost in the mists :
Truth must be sought with the Positivists.

β

Wise are their teachers beyond all comparison,
Comte, Huxley, Tyndall, Mill, Morley, and Harrison :
    Who will adventure to enter the lists
    With such a squadron of Positivists?

γ

Social arrangements are awful miscarriages ;
Cause of all crime is our system of marriages.
    Poets with sonnets and lovers with trysts
    Kindle the ire of the Positivists.

δ

Husbands and wives should be all one community,
Exquisite freedom with absolute unity.
    Wedding-rings worse are than manacled wrists—
    Such is the creed of the Positivists. ·

ε

There was an APE in the days that were earlier ;
Centuries passed, and his hair became curlier ;

Centuries more gave a thumb to his wrist—
Then he was MAN, and a Positivist.

ζ

If you are pious (mild form of insanity),
Bow down and worship the mass of Humanity.
Other religions are buried in mists
We're our own gods, say the Positivists.

EUELPIDES

These Positivists are very positive.

PEISTHETAIRUS.

And very negative too.   I can't agree
With folk who fancy they're their own creators.
Why they'd have made themselves a trifle handsomer,
With less of carrot-tress and spindle-shank,
To bring the girls about them.
                            Well, we've heard
The PROTOPLAST.   Who next?

EUELPIDES.

                     'Tis Mister GERM,

II

Who has set up in life as Sky-maker;
And thinks you'd like a ceiling for your City.

GERM.

I entertain no doubt a sky as vast   (*v*)
As ours, and quite as good to look at, could
Be formed from just the matter that one holds
Within a hollow palm.

PEISTHETAIRUS.

                By all the gods,
I'll have grand skies above me, Sky-maker!
If you say truth, I'll have no misty days
That look as dull as dirty ditchwater.
I'll have Claude sunrises and Turner sunsets,
And Canaletti noons and great Olympian
Days, such as Homer's gods enjoyed long since...
How long, the new gods perhaps may know...if not
The commentators on Theology,
Who help our Speaker with a commentary.

CHORUS.

α

Take just a trifling handful, O philosopher!
Of magic matter : give it a slight toss over

The ambient æther...and I don't see why
You shouldn't make a sky.

β

O hours Eutopian which we may anticipate!
Thick London fog how easy 'tis to dissipate,
And make the most pea-soupy day as clear
As Bass's brightest beer!

γ

Poet professor! Now my brain thou kindlest :
I am become a most determined Tyndallist.
If it is known a fellow can make skies,
Why not make bright blue eyes?

δ

This to deny, the folly of a dunce it is :
Surely a girl as easy as a sunset is.
If you can make a halo or eclipse,
Why not two laughing lips?

ε

The creed of Archimedes, erst of Sicily

And of D'Israëli ... *forti nil difficile* ...
 Is likewise mine.   Pygmalion was a fool
      Who should have gone to school.

ς

Why should an author scribble rhymes or articles?
Bring me a dozen tiny Tyndall-particles :
 Therefrom I'll coin a dinner, Nash's wine,
      And a nice girl to dine.

EUELPIDES.

What an idea!   Surely the Professor
Will make a fortune by his particles.
They'll be the pills of the age, and beat old Parr,
The sapient Holloway, the dyspeptic Cockle.
Fancy a pill-box that when opened carefully
Emitted a good dinner and good wine,
And somebody to help you eat and drink.

PEISTHETAIRUS.

I hope he has secured a patent.   But
We are wasting time.   Who is the next philosopher?

GORILLA.

" *Eras mus*," some one said unto Erasmus

Darwin : it seemed a kind of cataplasmus.

My grandfather, though rather too poetic,

Plaguing a prosy age with verse emetic,

Was not an absolute fool.   His name were dear,

But for George Canning and John Hookham Frere.(ξ)

I like my grandfather; I like the way

In which he made the roses go astray,

And made the modest old ranunculus flighty,

And turned the lily into Aphrodite.

I trace myself with rigorous logic ; for

I do maintain he was my ancestor.

And all impartial minds it seems to strike,

His likenesses are very monkey-like...

While, when a lady came, it seemed to strike her,

My portrait was a little monkey-liker.

So say I : "Whatsoe'er your brain or shape,

I am your father ... the Ancestral Ape."

EUELPIDES.

You say that I'm an Ape?   Then say your prayers :

·I'll kick you down the sky's unclimbable stairs !

Ah, folly makes mirth among children of earth—
A people whose birth was a glorious genesis :
They're sadly afraid of the likeness God made,
Take shape from the Ape, and say, " Ne'er was such
    pen as his !
He proves that we city men, wise men, and witty men,
Our spouses superb, and our babies soft-fingered,
Though we dwell in swell villas, are really gorillas,
Whose tails disappeared as the centuries lingered.
Ay, Apes are we all on this whirligig ball,
The big and the small, the dumpy and tall,
And especially those we illustrious call,
Whom we worship when powerful and kick when they
    fall."   -
That's the phrase in these days, though not openly
    said,
And the mad bad Rad cad, with the sad stupid head,
Is the Ass that likes kicking the Lion that's dead.
And the villanous quadruped deems it no sin
The cave to go in, and to strip off the skin
Of the glorious king of the wild forest-kin,

And to clothe his ridiculous body therein,

And come out and bray with a barbarous din...

Unmistakable absolute asinine yell,

That serveth full well of the Donkey to tell ;

He brays, "I am Lion ! I know how to roar ! "

But Farmer Giles swears, " I've heard *that* voice
before : "

And a stout oaken cudgel is tried on a hide

That cudgels beside have for centuries tried.

'Tis the way with the Ass and the Mob and the
Mass...

They'll bray the next day, whatsoe'er come to pass ;

And the bray will be louder, the tail will be prouder,

If you flatter their follies, and show them some quarter.

" A fool's still a fool, though he's brayed in a mortar."

God has said, if a myriad old records are true,

" In my likeness, ye lords of the Earth, I make you.

Go forth : live and love : to both liver and lover

There's a manifold multiplex world to discover.

There's a great commonwealth, which I yield you at
once :

There's an open career for both poet and dunce.

For you the birds flutter, and rich music utter...

For you wheat and kine yield divine bread and
   butter...

For you wine is hidden in grapes unforbidden,

For you there are swift-footed steeds to be ridden ;

In the womb of the earth there are gold, coal, and
   iron,

And diamonds light-flashing fair brows to environ,

And to clasp on slim wrists wine-drencht amethysts,

And rubies a flood of the essence of blood...

They are all in this mud.   Ye can all have your will,

But don't invent printing and don't make me ill."   (*o*)

Well, what's the reply of the Masters of Earth,

Endowed with the worth of a glorious birth,

Endowed with a likeness to Him who is All,

And absolute lords of the wandering ball,

Which, based upon granite, a fair virgin planet

Might sue for divorce, if Penzance could but scan it.

The material answer no oneiromancer

Could have guessed.   It was this : "We must rule by
   majorities,

For number and slumber and lumber encumber
Our thoughts, and our prayers are for Mayors and
    Authorities.
As ample requital we'll give you a title ...
Call you Brahm, Vishnu, Zeus, or Jehovah—what not?
And we'll make for our need each a different creed,
And we'll doom disbelievers to something that's hot.
But we really must stick to our natural shapes ...
We ape one the other in muslins or crapes,
In our mud of dull cities we're anxious to trapse :
You would turn us to Gods.   We prefer to be Apes."

SEWING MACHINE, ESQ.

God's the one being that can have no will.   (π)
We are machines : machines are more than we.
Would men were half as useful, half as admirable.
When I find man creating a machine,
To cut up postage-stamps, weigh sovereigns,
Or thrash out wheat, or take a photograph,
I think 'twould be the highest compliment
To say he was as great as his machine.
Let us abandon every egoïsm :

I

Our normal evolution is to be
Organs of reason, implements of justice.
If malformation stop not th' evolution,
He will ascend [I don't know who *He* is]
From Destiny's last coil of spiral groove.
Where Dr. Anagke wields the horrid birch,
To the resplendent circle of ideals
And passions, weaving lovely magical chains.

CHORUS.

α

That's the philosopher! T'others we'll toss over
 Into the still silent sapphire abyss;
He's the man all puzzles to cross over.
   Wisdom is his.

β

Heaven, sky, and earth are fine pieces of.scenery:
 God is a Being without any will:
Man is a mortal machine whose machinery
   Outdoes him still.

γ

Great theologians, talk not of Trinity ;
    Heretics, plague us no more with your fibs :
One question only, which is the Divinity,
        Wilcox or Gibbs ?

δ

SEWING MACHINE, Esquire, writes so deliciously,
    Writes on such fine ungrammatical plan,
That we're disposed just to question, suspiciously,
    ... " *Can he be man ?* "

ε

What we suspect, in this wondrously wise cycle,
    When such queer notions some people of nous
        trap,
Is that his noble Papa was a Bicycle ...
        Mother a Mousetrap.

ζ

When the two lovers were welded in marriage,
    They were desirous that no one should know, so

They, when their heir came, mankind to disparage,
.Christened him SEW SO.

η

Ethics of Will, without ethics or will,
     Prove, poor MACHINE, and grow duncer and
          duncer;
Write in vile words viler nonsense...but still
          Man is God's son, sir.

PEISTHETAIRUS.

Well, it appears to me that PROTOPLAST
And GERM are far too brilliant for our City;
While birds would naturally object to seeing
GORILLA throned within our Academus,
Peripatetic, philosophic, prolix :
Wherefore I think that I must recommend
To the Town Council of Cloud-Cuckoo-Town
SEWING MACHINE as teacher of philosophy.
He's a safe guide; he quite ignores absurdity,
And sends his needle through the gaps of time,
Darning them thoroughly; hem-stitches heaven,

Cuts out the gussets of earth, sews straighter seams
Than any other machine as yet invented.
You see at once his needles never break,
Or if they do, are easily replaced.
Yes, he must be our teacher.

EUELPIDES.

Master, see !
Some gentlemen are coming up from Earth,
Upon an evident embassy.

PEISTHETAIRUS.

Let them come.
An aëritory's better than a territory ;
They can't invade us here with mitrailleuses,
Field guns, or ironclads.   Pray introduce them.

EUELPIDES.

Messrs. Laetuslapis, Bisnotus, and Lachrimae.

PEISTHETAIRUS.

Gentlemen, welcome to our unbuilt city,

Which is to be metropolis of three worlds,
Richer than London, drudging slave of cities,
Stronger than Berlin, fiercest fiend of cities,
Gayer than Paris, harlot among cities :
Here we shall have all glory of earth and sky,
But neither smoke nor gold : here shall we have
Power to destroy invasion instantly,
And therefore perfect peace : here shall we have
True beauty, true delight, true love, true light,
And therefore no hysterical excitement.
These things I mention as preliminaries,
Just to prevent misunderstanding   Now
I shall be glad to listen.

LAETUSLAPIS.

                    You are courteous,
And we most cordially thank you.   Three
Courses are open to the realm I govern...
Either to be your ally and never help you,
Or else your enemy and never fight you,
Or else entirely neutral : which do you
Prefer ?

EUELPIDES.

His Highness Peisthetairus wishes
To answer all ambassadors together.
[*Aside*] (Besides, the Chorus are away at dinner).

BISNOTUS.

I am deputed by my Emperor
To say he cannot let a State arise
On the other bank of the great River Air :
Still, if you will be tributary allies,
And help us stanchly in our coming wars,
Sending your eagles to peck out the eyes
Of enemies, your magpies and your jackdaws
To steal their letters, and your crows and vultures
To eat their bodies, we may tolerate you,
At an amount of tribute to be fixed
By a committee to be chosen by me.

EUELPIDES.

That gentleman is very liberal ;
His Emperor will blow him up for offering
Such generous terms.

LACHRIMAE.

        One thing have I to say :
We are old enemies and old allies :
We kneel in worship to the Cock that crows
For no conceivable reason every hour...
He being ornithic reflex of ourselves :
We eat you greedily and dress you better
Than any other nation upon earth
Which being so, let us conclude a treaty
Offensive and defensive.

EUELPIDES.

             That old gentleman
Is rather cool.

PEISTHETAIRUS.

I think we'll hear the Chorus
If they have finished their infallible meal.

CHORUS.

α

O Laetuslapis ! your triform shape is
    As odd as Cerberus or Scylla :

The Master maintains that, though you have brains,
    He'd prefer for ally a stanch gorilla.

β

Bumptious Bisnotus! we'll here eat lotos,
    Careless whether you threaten or wheedle.
In the Realm of Air we need have no care
    About mitrailleuses and guns of needle.

γ

Great Lachrimae! a Power you'll be
    For a year (or a day) if you're wise and witty.
But a treaty with you would hardly do :
    For where will you be when we've built our City ?

PEISTHETAIRUS.

The oracle has spoken, gentlemen.
That is the voice of many myriad birds,
Who in poetic committee dealt with you,
And turned their resolutions into song.
You represent three nations and three capitals :
One nation ox-like and the city huge,

One nation barbarous and the city slow,
One nation frivolous and the city gay.
You cannot well be close allies of ours :
Our nation is poetic, every bird ...
Our city will be joyous, musical, pure.
The world has never seen such city yet.

[Exeunt statesmen.

[Enter TOM TIT, *flying with immense swiftness.*

TOM TIT.

Good news! The City's finished.

PEISTHETAIRUS.

Finished! Why
No one's been asked to lay the foundation stone,
And knight somebody. This is impertinence.
Who finished it, you coloured feathered atom?

TOM TIT.

The royal family of the Rocs, who rule
In Airland. They are no degenerate birds,
And our great King has seventy thousand sons,

Grandsons, great-grandsons.   Uninstructed mortals
Puzzle themselves about the Pyramids,
And sage astronomers attempt to give them
A scientific meaning.   Utter nonsense!
Some young Rocs built them in their babyhood,
When they were sent for change of air to Egypt
(Centuries before the Deluge, Bunsen thinks);
It took them all a summer afternoon,
And they were late to tea.
                              Stonehenge, again,
Whose structure seems enormous to you mortals,
And of appalling age, was just put up,
Twenty or thirty centuries ago,
To shelter from the rain some lady-Rocs,
Who had come out upon a picnic party,
Not knowing the dampness of your wretched island.

PEISTHETAIRUS.

Go on, you tiny braggart.

TOM TIT.

So the Rocs,

K 2

Knowing their father wished a city built,
A city of glory, beauty, permanence,
A city worthy of this Realm of Air,
In which no dirt can dwell, no weakness live,
No ugliness exist—a city worthy
Of the great Nation of Birds, the only winged
And song-possessing and world-traversing creatures—
Thought they would build it while he was at dinner.
So off they flew, full seventy thousand strong,
To the Valley of Diamonds, and brought thence great
    blocks
Of the mere stones that for strange reasons gladden
Maidens and madden matrons and sometimes sadden
Husbands and fathers when the bills come in.
So the walls are of undying adamant,
With courses here and there of keen sea-sapphire,
Blood-ruby, emerald of darkest green,
And now and again a fretwork of pure pearls,
Which all Caÿster's fishing splashing birds
Found out by opening all the oldest oysters
That had lain hid in the primeval sludge
Deposited when earth was made.   Moreover,

Prince Roc, the eldest born, and strongest, wisest,
Flew off to the central city of the Sun,
And brought from burning Heliopolis
A mighty obelisk of living light,
Which from the omphalos of Cloud-Cuckoo-Town
Points upward many a mile.

PEISTHETAIRUS.

It can't be true.

TOM TIT.

Pray come and see. The King is coming down—
Cross rather, for the minstrel-Nightingale,
Instead of singing tune to royal slumber,
Sang while his sons were doing masons' work.

[PEISTHETAIRUS *meets* KING ROC *at the city-gate.*

KING ROC.

You see what birds can do. Still you were architect,
And well deserved the usual five per cent.
Now shall we try whether we can defy
Both dwellers on our frontiers, gods and men,

And teach them both a nobler way to live.
See the great sunset on the obelisk spire,
And burning through the diamond battlements,
And colouring through us the world beneath,
Where at this moment many a happy lover
Is wandering with his sweetheart.   Perfect Procne,
Sing for the City and its King.

PROCNE.

α

This is Air's sweet City
    Builded by the birds,
And I sing a ditty
    More of sound than words ...
Pure voice of purest æther that this planet girds.

CHORUS.

I'd rather hear the bleating of flocks and lowing of
herds.

PROCNE.

β

Sunsets now will glisten
    Brighter than before :

Children now will listen
On the wild west shore
For vesper music sweeter than any heard of yore.

CHORUS.

Still Procne, when she keeps one awake, becomes a
bore.

PROCNE.

γ

Look up, wandering lover
To the sunset sky!
Can you not discover
With visionary eye,
A river in the heavens, great mansions built thereby?

CHORUS.

I hope the rents are not uncomfortably high.

PROCNE.

δ

Here all dreams have vanished
Which 'mid fools prevail :

Vices all are banished
  Beyond our radiant pale.
We live and love and sing and through clear æther
  sail.

CHORUS.

But is there not a corner to find one's cakes and ale?

PROCNE.

ε

Happy when we wander,
  Happy in our nests,
Never do we ponder
  Of the Fates' behests:
Our life flies through wide space, our love on soft
  moss rests.

CHORUS.

A strange philosophy this song-bird manifests!

PROCNE.

ζ

O to pierce the zenith
  Which no steps have trod,

Where the bird's eye kenneth
Marvellous touch of God—
And then to flutter down on dew-cooled emerald sod!

CHORUS.

Birds seem more wise than men in some things. Very
odd !

PROCNE.

η

O the sphere to girdle,
Voyage like a dream ;
See the keen ice curdle,
See bright oceans gleam,
Look down on mighty cities that mere toy - towns
seem.

CHORUS.

Well, if I were a bird I'd never go by steam.

PROCNE.

θ

We can dart, drift, dally,
Dream upon the wing,

L

Woo in woodland valley,
Twitter, chatter, sing :
For very joy we live, and for no other thing.

CHORUS.

Men, being more unwise, to toil and trouble cling.

PROCNE.

ı

Now our City's founded,
On the virgin verge
Of the sky, and bounded
By the cloudy surge —
So into civic life we suddenly emerge.

CHORUS.

I'd like to be a bird and from an egg emerge.

PROCNE.

x

In our Town reign beauty,
Peace, and love, and song ;

Never any duty
Since never any wrong :
Nor fear, because air-dwellers are always safe and
strong.

CHORUS.

I'll get a suit of feathers and to the birds belong.

PROCNE (*retreating*).

λ

Deeper still and deeper,
Into air I go.
Dream, O loving sleeper,
And dream of love, for lo
Thy dream shall be fulfilled, since Procne tells thee
so.

CHORUS.

Far flies the musical bird into the sunset-glow!

NOTES.

α. Mr. Hawkins, the most easy of forensic wits, may possibly understand this allusion.

β. Tennyson.

γ. ἄγε σύννομέ μοι, κ.τ.λ.

δ. Often, on summer nights in Berks.

ε. "The different seabirds, and the birds that bore
The Asian marsh of sweet Caÿster's shore,
With copious dews their bustling shoulders lave,
And duck their heads beneath the curling wave,
Then deeper still into the breakers dash,
And wanton in the luxury of splash."
BLACKMORE, Georgics, vv. 444–9.

ζ.   ἐποποποτοποποποποποῖ,
    ἰω ἰω, ἰτὼ ἰτὼ ἰτὼ ἰτὼ.

η. This fact ornithic I can aver from my experience of a pair of pet owls, who like nothing better than to have their feathered eyelids scratched. I see one of them at this moment through thick-falling snow (23rd of March, 1872) realizing Keats's most Shakespearian line :
"The owl, for all his feathers, was a-cold."

θ. Violet, Indigo, Blue, Green, Yellow, Orange, Red.

ι. I fear it was *Jenny* in the poem, for *guinea* was supposed to rhyme with it : but any flighty name may suit a Lovelily.

κ. Nine + three.

λ. "History of English Rhythms." Pickering.

μ. "Anlipig aldormon."—Saxon Chronicle, Parker MS., A.D. 1871.

ν. *Vide* Professor Tyndall's Lecture on Sky-making.

ξ. *Vide* "Loves of the Triangles," a mathematical and philosophical poem, inscribed to Dr. Darwin.—*Anti-Jacobin*, April 16th, 1798.

ο. Doctor Faustus has been uniformly sent *ad diabolum* by the poets for his invention of printing.

π. *Vide* a recent utterance of Mr. Moncure Conway's.

Wyman & Sons, Printers, Great Queen Street, London, W.C.